·TELL ME ABOUT·
WINGS, WHEELS & SAILS

By Tom Stacy
Illustrated by Peter Bull

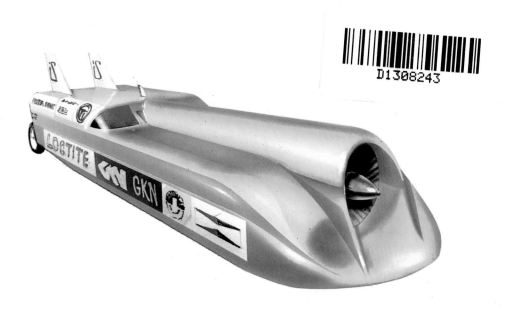

RANDOM HOUSE   NEW YORK

Contents

First American edition, 1991

Copyright © 1990 by Grisewood & Dempsey. All rights reserved under International and Pan-American Copyright Conventions. Published in the United States by Random House, Inc., New York. Originally published in Great Britain by Kingfisher Books, a Grisewood & Dempsey Company, in 1990.

Library of Congress Cataloging-in-Publication Data
Stacy, Tom.
    Wings, wheels & sails / by Tom Stacy; illustrated by Peter Bull [et at.].
        p.   cm.—(Tell me about)
    Includes index.
    Summary: Questions and answers address the many ways in which humans move from place to place, examining airplanes, cars, trains, bicycles, and other forms of transportation.
    ISBN 0-679-80863-9
    1. Transportation—Juvenile literature.
[1. Transportation—Miscellanea. 2. Questions and answers.] I. Bull, Peter, ill. II. Title. III. Title: Wings, wheels, and sails. IV. Series.
TA1149.S72 1991
629.04—dc20   90-42977
                                          CIP
                                           AC

Manufactured in Spain   1 2 3 4 5 6 7 8 9 10

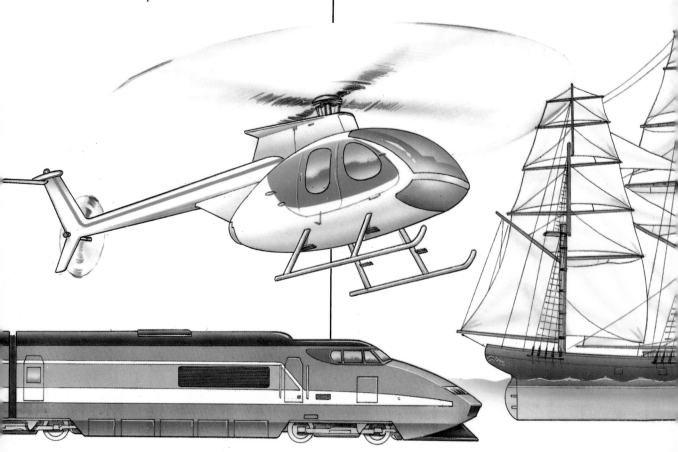

How fast can airplanes fly?

Faster and faster planes have been built since the first powered flights took place early this century. Today, the record for the world's fastest jet plane is still held by the USA's Lockheed SR-71A. In 1976, it flew 2,193 miles per hour (mph).

The world's fastest planes are powered by rocket engines — only space rockets can fly faster. In 1967, the USA's X-15 rocket plane flew 4,534 mph!

DO YOU KNOW

The speed of sound slowly drops with height above sea level, but above about 36,000 feet it stays the same. It's around 760 mph at sea level, and about 660 mph above 36,000 feet. A plane flying at the speed of sound is at Mach 1. Twice the speed of sound is Mach 2, and so on.

The USA's X-15 (above) remains the fastest plane ever made. Its rocket engine propels it to nearly seven times the speed of sound.

The first plane to fly faster than the speed of sound in level flight was the USA's rocket plane, the Bell X-1 (above), in 1947.

The jet-engined Anglo-French Concorde (above) is the world's only supersonic passenger plane. Its cruising speed is 1,445 mph.

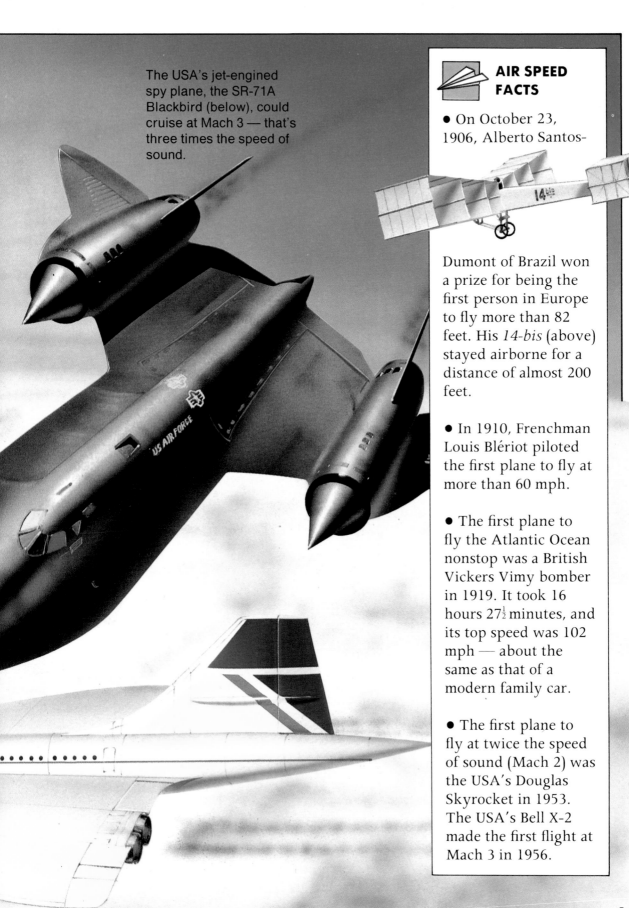

The USA's jet-engined spy plane, the SR-71A Blackbird (below), could cruise at Mach 3 — that's three times the speed of sound.

US AIR FORCE

AIR SPEED FACTS

● On October 23, 1906, Alberto Santos-

14-bis

Dumont of Brazil won a prize for being the first person in Europe to fly more than 82 feet. His *14-bis* (above) stayed airborne for a distance of almost 200 feet.

● In 1910, Frenchman Louis Blériot piloted the first plane to fly at more than 60 mph.

● The first plane to fly the Atlantic Ocean nonstop was a British Vickers Vimy bomber in 1919. It took 16 hours $27\frac{1}{2}$ minutes, and its top speed was 102 mph — about the same as that of a modern family car.

● The first plane to fly at twice the speed of sound (Mach 2) was the USA's Douglas Skyrocket in 1953. The USA's Bell X-2 made the first flight at Mach 3 in 1956.

Which is the biggest airplane?

The world's largest passenger plane is the USA's Boeing 747, or jumbo jet. It is 230 feet long and weighs nearly 350 tons. The heaviest plane is the USSR's Antonov An-225, which weighs 560 tons.

JUMBO FACTS

● In 1989, a QANTAS Boeing 747-400 flew nonstop from London, England, to Sydney, Australia, in a record 20 hours.

The body of a plane is called the fuselage. Inside the 747's fuselage is the passenger cabin, with seating for nearly 400 people.

The 747's wings measure 200 feet from tip to tip. The plane has four jet engines, mounted two beneath each wing.

The flight deck is where the captain and co-pilot sit. There is also an automatic pilot — a computer that can fly the plane.

PILOT'S CODE

Every plane has a code name made up of letters and numbers. So that no one mixes up the sounds, pilots use the sound alphabet shown here to give these names over the radio. You could use it to send messages in code to your friends.

A Alfa
B Bravo
C Charlie
D Delta
E Echo
F Foxtrot
G Golf
H Hotel
I India
J Juliet
K Kilo
L Lima
M Mike
N November
O Oscar
P Papa
Q Quebec
R Romeo
S Sierra
T Tango
U Uniform
V Victor
W Whisky
X X-ray
Y Yankee
Z Zulu

Who flew the first airplane?

The first person to fly a plane was Orville Wright of the USA, on December 17, 1903. People had flown in balloons and gliders before this, but Orville Wright was the first person to fly a plane with an engine.

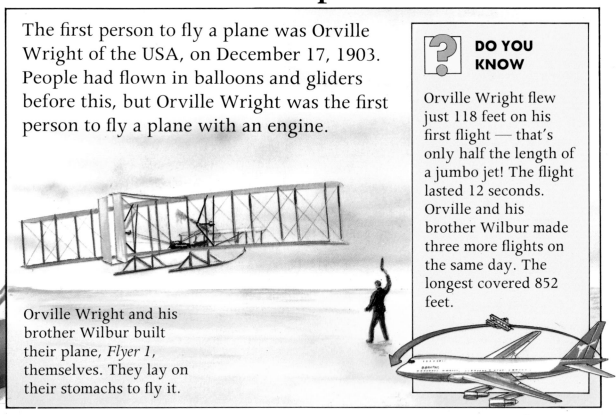

Orville Wright and his brother Wilbur built their plane, *Flyer 1*, themselves. They lay on their stomachs to fly it.

? DO YOU KNOW

Orville Wright flew just 118 feet on his first flight — that's only half the length of a jumbo jet! The flight lasted 12 seconds. Orville and his brother Wilbur made three more flights on the same day. The longest covered 852 feet.

Who flew around the world first?

The first planes to fly around the world were two US Douglas seaplanes in 1924. They took 175 days. US pilot Wiley Post made the first solo flight around the world in 1933. His plane (below) was called *Winnie Mae*, and in it he flew more than 15,500 miles in 7 days, 18 hours, and 49 minutes.

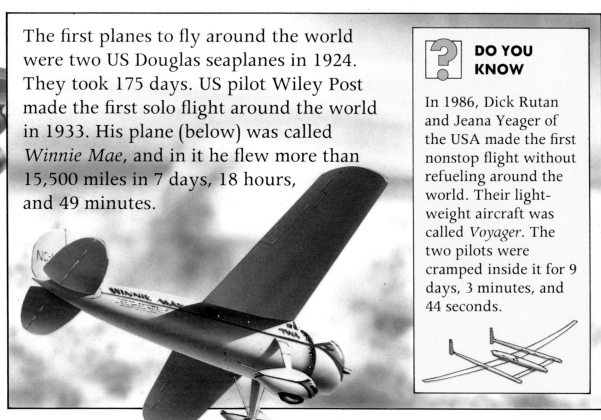

? DO YOU KNOW

In 1986, Dick Rutan and Jeana Yeager of the USA made the first nonstop flight without refueling around the world. Their light-weight aircraft was called *Voyager*. The two pilots were cramped inside it for 9 days, 3 minutes, and 44 seconds.

How do airplanes stay in the air?

Planes can't fly without wings. Wings must have a special shape called an airfoil, which is more curved above than below. Air flows faster over the airfoil's curved upper surface than beneath it. This creates a force called lift, which enables the plane to fly.

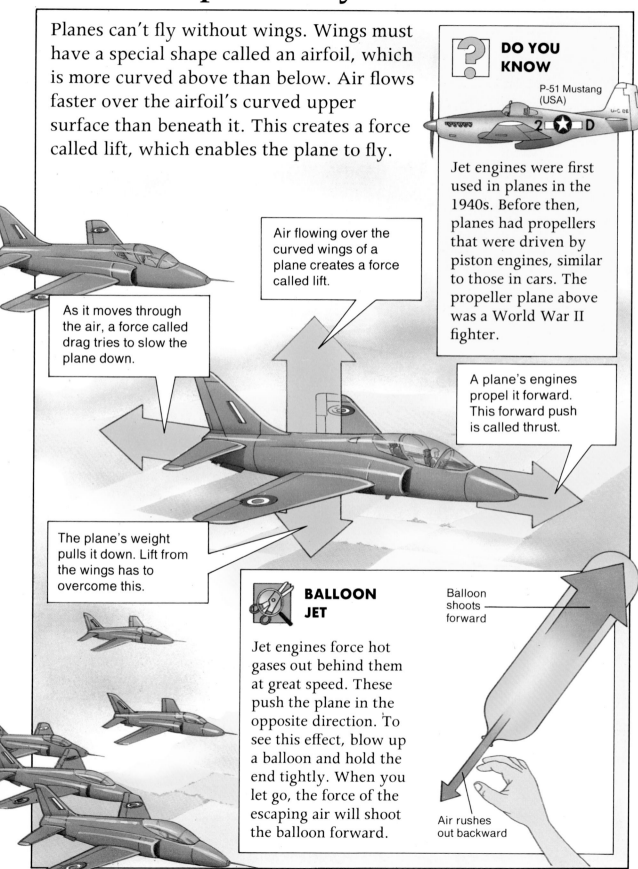

? DO YOU KNOW

P-51 Mustang (USA)

Jet engines were first used in planes in the 1940s. Before then, planes had propellers that were driven by piston engines, similar to those in cars. The propeller plane above was a World War II fighter.

Air flowing over the curved wings of a plane creates a force called lift.

As it moves through the air, a force called drag tries to slow the plane down.

A plane's engines propel it forward. This forward push is called thrust.

The plane's weight pulls it down. Lift from the wings has to overcome this.

BALLOON JET

Jet engines force hot gases out behind them at great speed. These push the plane in the opposite direction. To see this effect, blow up a balloon and hold the end tightly. When you let go, the force of the escaping air will shoot the balloon forward.

Balloon shoots forward

Air rushes out backward

8

How do gliders stay in the air?

Gliders are planes without engines. Like all planes, though, a glider will fly only if it is moving fast enough to keep air flowing over its wings, so that the lift is greater than its weight.

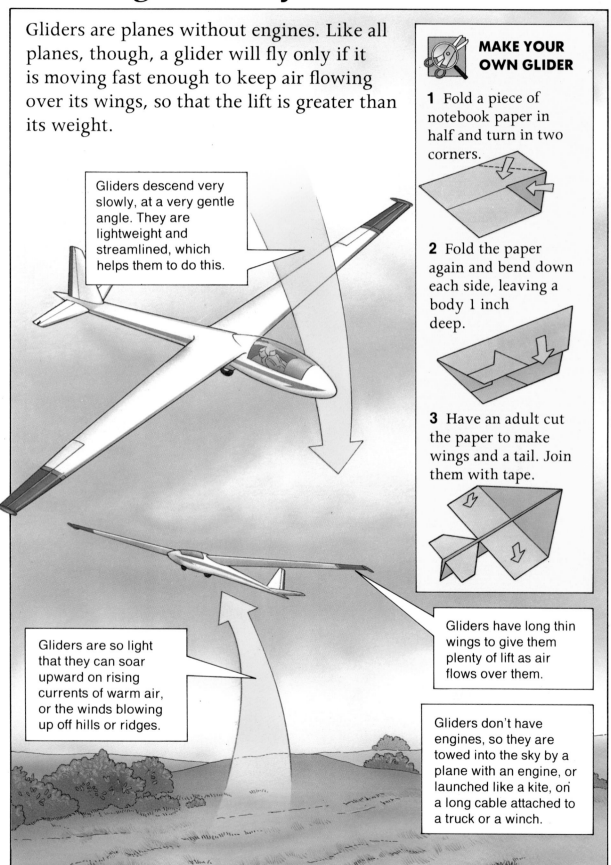

Gliders descend very slowly, at a very gentle angle. They are lightweight and streamlined, which helps them to do this.

Gliders are so light that they can soar upward on rising currents of warm air, or the winds blowing up off hills or ridges.

MAKE YOUR OWN GLIDER

1 Fold a piece of notebook paper in half and turn in two corners.

2 Fold the paper again and bend down each side, leaving a body 1 inch deep.

3 Have an adult cut the paper to make wings and a tail. Join them with tape.

Gliders have long thin wings to give them plenty of lift as air flows over them.

Gliders don't have engines, so they are towed into the sky by a plane with an engine, or launched like a kite, on a long cable attached to a truck or a winch.

How do helicopters fly?

Helicopters can hover in midair and fly in any direction — even backward! Instead of wings they have spinning blades called rotors, which act as wings and propellers to give lift and thrust. Helicopter pilots control their craft by changing the pitch, or angle, at which the rotor blades spin through the air.

Because they can hover and fly straight up or down, helicopters are especially useful for rescues at sea.

What are V/STOL jets?

V/STOL is short for "vertical/short take-off and landing" (*vertical* means straight up or down). The jet engines of V/STOL planes have nozzles that can be angled downward for take-off and landing. This allows V/STOL planes to fly straight up or down, just like helicopters do. V/STOL planes can also hover and fly backward.

The Harrier's engine has four nozzles. When they point backward, the jet thrust from them sends the plane forward.

The Harrier (right and below) was the world's first successful V/STOL jet. It began test flights in the late 1960s.

As well as hovering, V/STOL jets can match the speed of many other jet planes in forward flight.

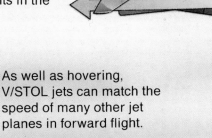

The Harrier can take off in more or less its own length. Large aircraft need a runway at least 5,000 feet long.

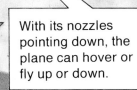

With its nozzles pointing down, the plane can hover or fly up or down.

❓ DO YOU KNOW

One of the earliest V/STOL planes was the Lockheed XFV-1 (below). It was built in the early 1950s. As well as normal forward take-offs, it could take off and land vertically. Unlike modern V/STOLs, it was positioned tail down and nose up to do this. The XFV-1 was difficult to fly, however, and the program was dropped.

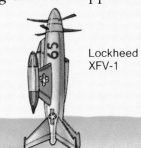

Lockheed XFV-1

How do balloons fly?

Balloons fly because they are lighter than the air around them. Warm air is lighter than cold air, so a balloon filled with hot air will rise. Some balloons are filled with gases that are lighter than air, such as helium.

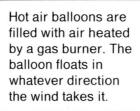

Hot air balloons are filled with air heated by a gas burner. The balloon floats in whatever direction the wind takes it.

To make the balloon descend, the pilot turns off the gas burner. This lets the air inside the balloon cool and get heavier.

 BALLOON FACTS

• The first balloon to carry living things was built in France by the two Montgolfier brothers, and launched in 1783. A sheep, a duck, and a rooster flew in the balloon's basket and landed safely after 8 minutes.

• The first people to fly in a balloon were François Pilâtre de Rozier and the Marquis d'Arlandes. In 1783, they flew across Paris for 25 minutes.

• The highest flight for a balloon carrying people is 113,740 feet (1961).

Concorde — 50,000 feet

Mt. Everest — 29,028 feet

What are airships?

Airships are large balloons with engines. The engines give them enough power to fly in any direction, even into the wind.

The first successful airship flew in 1852. In the 1920s and 1930s, airships were used as long-distance airliners to carry passengers. Unfortunately they were filled with hydrogen gas, which catches fire easily, and several were destroyed by terrible fires.

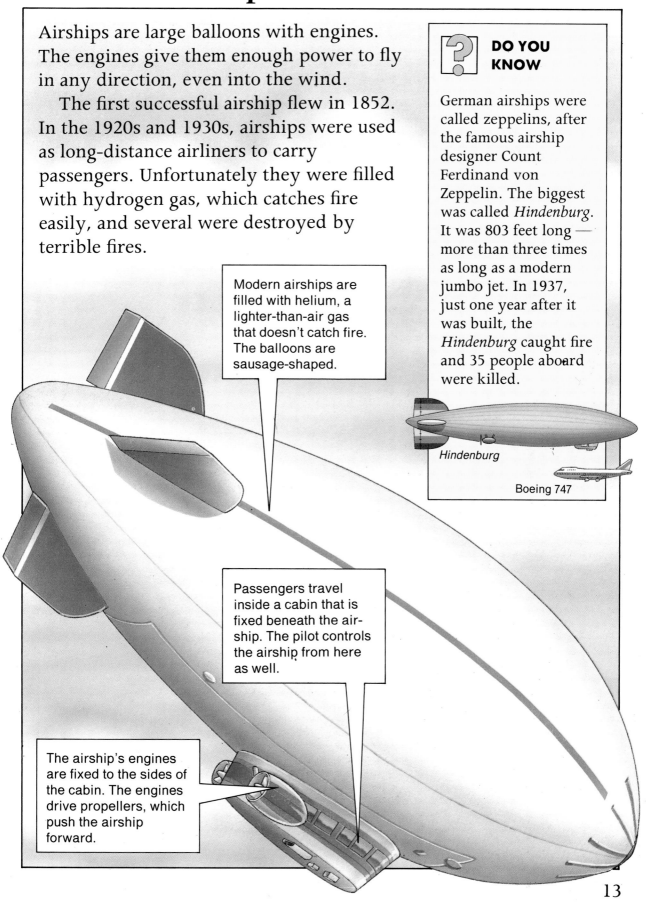

? DO YOU KNOW

German airships were called zeppelins, after the famous airship designer Count Ferdinand von Zeppelin. The biggest was called *Hindenburg*. It was 803 feet long — more than three times as long as a modern jumbo jet. In 1937, just one year after it was built, the *Hindenburg* caught fire and 35 people aboard were killed.

Hindenburg

Boeing 747

Modern airships are filled with helium, a lighter-than-air gas that doesn't catch fire. The balloons are sausage-shaped.

Passengers travel inside a cabin that is fixed beneath the airship. The pilot controls the airship from here as well.

The airship's engines are fixed to the sides of the cabin. The engines drive propellers, which push the airship forward.

Which is the fastest car?

The world land speed record for a car is just over 633 mph — that's faster than many jet airliners can fly. It's held by the British car Thrust 2, which is propelled by the thrust from an aircraft jet engine. Because ordinary cars are powered by engines that drive the wheels around, they can't go as fast as jet or rocket cars. The top speed for a wheel-driven car is 429 mph.

? DO YOU KNOW

The wheel was invented about 6,000 years ago. Before this, tree trunks were used as rollers to move heavy objects. Someone watching a roller turn probably thought of the wheel.

1 In 1899 the battery-powered *La Jamais Contente* (left) was the first car to go faster than 60 mph.

2 Henry Segrave's Sunbeam car (below) set a record of 203.80 mph in 1927.

3 The first car to go faster than 300 mph was John Cobb's Railton (below), in 1947.

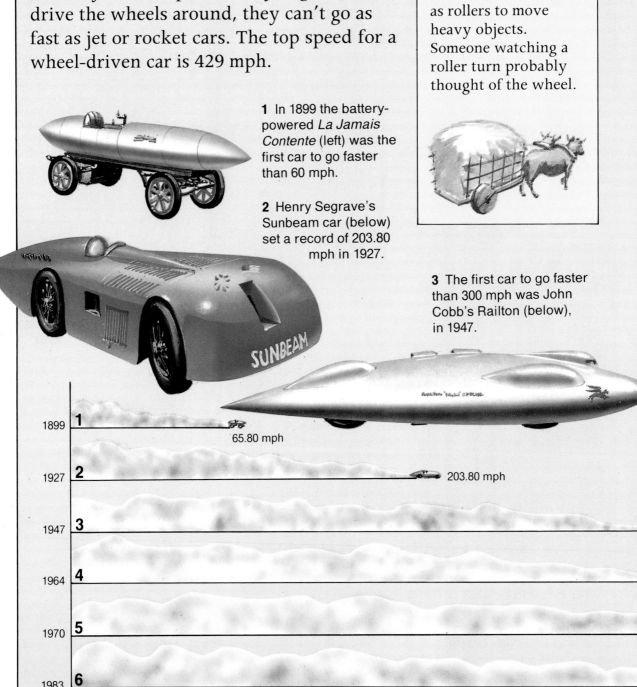

1899 **1**	65.80 mph
1927 **2**	203.80 mph
1947 **3**	
1964 **4**	
1970 **5**	
1983 **6**	

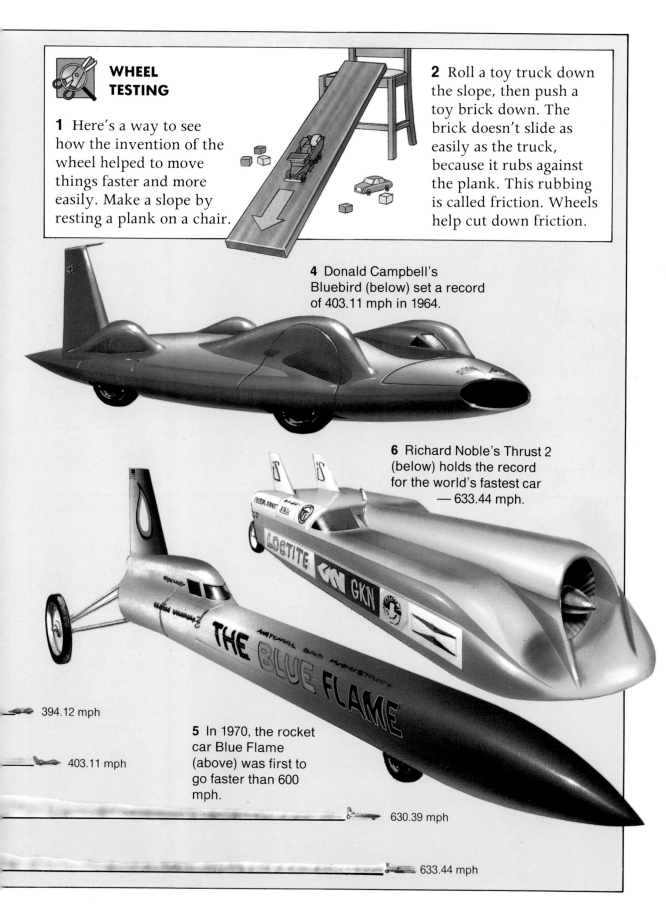

WHEEL TESTING

1 Here's a way to see how the invention of the wheel helped to move things faster and more easily. Make a slope by resting a plank on a chair.

2 Roll a toy truck down the slope, then push a toy brick down. The brick doesn't slide as easily as the truck, because it rubs against the plank. This rubbing is called friction. Wheels help cut down friction.

4 Donald Campbell's Bluebird (below) set a record of 403.11 mph in 1964.

6 Richard Noble's Thrust 2 (below) holds the record for the world's fastest car — 633.44 mph.

394.12 mph

403.11 mph

5 In 1970, the rocket car Blue Flame (above) was first to go faster than 600 mph.

630.39 mph

633.44 mph

Which is the most popular car?

More Volkswagen Beetles have been made than any other car — by the time European production stopped in 1978, over 20 million had been sold. The first Beetles were made in Germany in 1938. The German word *volkswagen* means "people's car."

? DO YOU KNOW

Ferrari cars from Italy have been sold at auction for $10 million, making them the world's most expensive second-hand cars.

The Beetle was designed in the mid-1930s by an Austrian engineer named Ferdinand Porsche. The car on the left is a 1952 model. Early models didn't have rear windows.

Which is the biggest car?

The biggest cars ever made were the Bugatti Royales of 1927. They were over 22 feet long and weighed nearly 3 tons. Only a few Bugatti Royales were built — in 1986, a bidder at an auction paid over $8 million for one of them!

? DO YOU KNOW

The world's longest car was built in the USA in 1982. It was 72 feet long and had 18 wheels. It even had its own swimming pool!

Who invented the automobile?

The earliest powered road vehicle was built in 1769 and had a steam engine. But the first true automobile — with a gasoline engine — was made by Karl Benz of Germany in 1885. Benz's car had three wheels and looked like a large tricycle. Another German, Gottlieb Daimler, built a four-wheeled car in 1886.

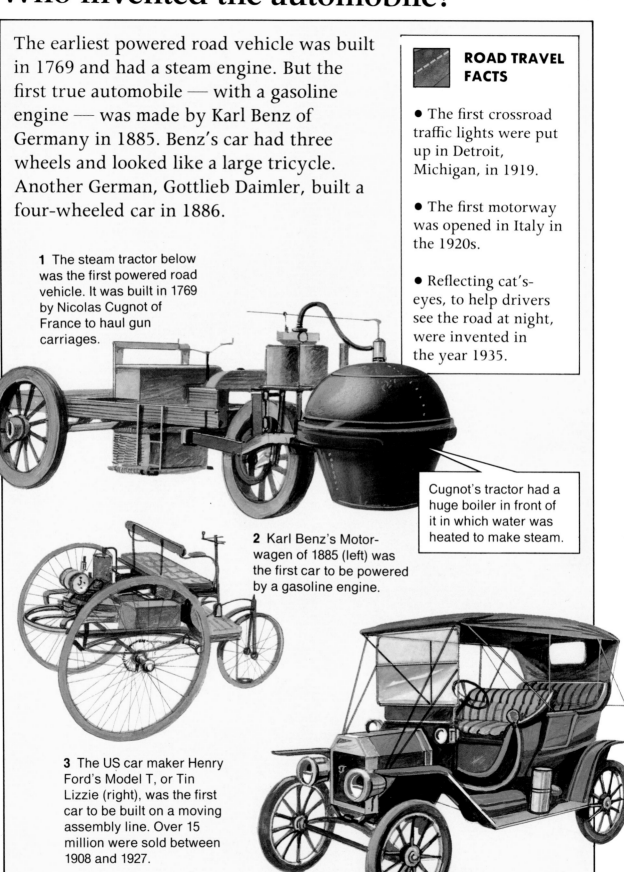

1 The steam tractor below was the first powered road vehicle. It was built in 1769 by Nicolas Cugnot of France to haul gun carriages.

Cugnot's tractor had a huge boiler in front of it in which water was heated to make steam.

2 Karl Benz's Motor-wagen of 1885 (left) was the first car to be powered by a gasoline engine.

3 The US car maker Henry Ford's Model T, or Tin Lizzie (right), was the first car to be built on a moving assembly line. Over 15 million were sold between 1908 and 1927.

How are cars made?

Cars are put together in factories, on assembly lines. First, though, the body parts are cut and shaped from sheets of metal by huge machines. The parts are then welded together to make the body. After this is painted, working parts such as the engine and gearbox are fitted. Finally, seats, windows, and wheels are added, and the car is driven off for testing.

The shell, or empty car body, is placed on the beginning of the assembly line.

In many factories, much of the welding and fitting is done by robots.

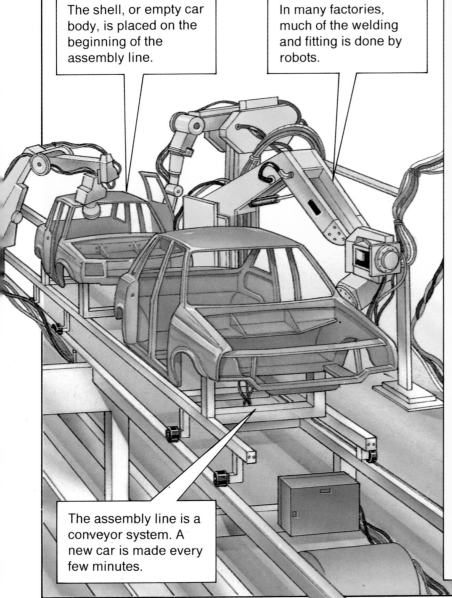

The assembly line is a conveyor system. A new car is made every few minutes.

How are cars tested?

Every newly made car is tested at the factory to make sure it works properly. All the parts are checked, and the finished car is approved by an inspector. New car designs are tested even more thoroughly, going through months of trials before production begins. Cars are always crash-tested to see how strong and safe they are.

To see what happens in a crash, a test car with a dummy driver is propelled into a wall. These tests help people to design stronger, safer cars.

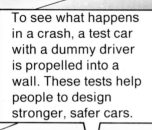

Speed track tests show car makers how well the engine works, how fast the car can go, and how safe it is traveling at high speed.

LAWS OF MOTION

If a car hits something, the passengers are thrown forward. If they aren't wearing seat belts, they may even be flung out of the car. This is because things that are already moving tend to keep going — scientists call this effect inertia. Here's a way to see inertia in action for yourself.

Load a toy truck with toy bricks. Push the truck so that it crashes into something. The truck stops, but inertia makes the bricks keep on moving.

Truck stops

Bricks keep moving

Which is the world's longest road race?

First held in 1923, France's Le Mans race lasts for 24 hours and covers a distance of about 3,300 miles. The cars reach a top speed of nearly 240 mph along the straightest part of the course. The winner is the car that travels farthest in 24 hours.

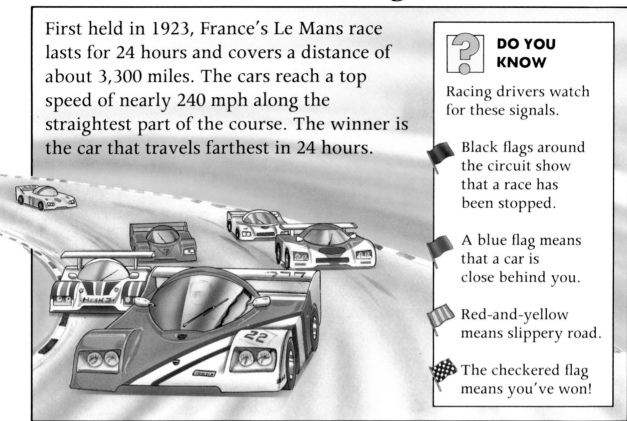

Where is the world's longest road?

The Pan-American Highway is the world's longest road system. It covers 29,516 miles, east-west and north-south. It starts at the northern border of Mexico and stretches almost to the tip of South America.

Surface — concrete or asphalt

Base — concrete, stone, or asphalt

Road bed — rock or soil

What is a tandem?

A tandem is a long truck-trailer combination — a large powerful truck pulling two or more big trailers loaded with cargo. They are often used in parts of a country where there are no railways. In Australia, for example, tandems are used to transport animals from remote sheep or cattle farms.

When were bicycles invented?

The earliest bicycles, called dandy-horses, appeared in the 1790s. They didn't have pedals — riders pushed themselves along with their feet. The first pedal bicycle was made by a Scot named Kirkpatrick Macmillan in 1839. The first modern-looking bicycle was the *vélocipède* made by Pierre Michaux of France in 1861.

1 Dandy-horses (right) were invented in France in the 1790s. Moving themselves along with their feet, riders could reach speeds of 9 mph.

2 The *vélocipède* (below), or bone-shaker, was invented in 1861. It was the first bicycle with a brake. It didn't have a chain or gears, though — the pedals turned the front wheel.

4 The first bicycle with pedals linked by a chain to the back wheel appeared in the 1880s. Gears were invented in the 1900s — modern bicycles (right) can have anything from 5 to 21 gears.

Gears make cycling easier. In low gear, the rear wheel turns more slowly than the pedals, giving more power for starts and hills. In high gear, the wheels turn much faster than the pedals.

3 The highwheeler (above) was invented in 1870. To climb on, riders used a small step just above the back wheel. Once moving, they could reach speeds of more than 18 mph.

Which is the fastest motorcycle?

The Kawasaki ZZ-R1100 (below) is one of the world's fastest road bikes. In tests, this Japanese motorcycle has gone more than 175 mph. Racing bikes can go even faster, however, and reach speeds greater than 185 mph.

The first motorcycle with a gasoline engine was called the *Einspur*. It was made in Germany in 1885 by Gottlieb Daimler and Wilhelm Maybach.

MOTORCYCLE FACTS

● The *Einspur* (below) was the first motorcycle. Everything but the engine was made of wood. Its top speed was 11.8 mph.

● By the 1930s, motorcycles could travel faster than 120 mph.

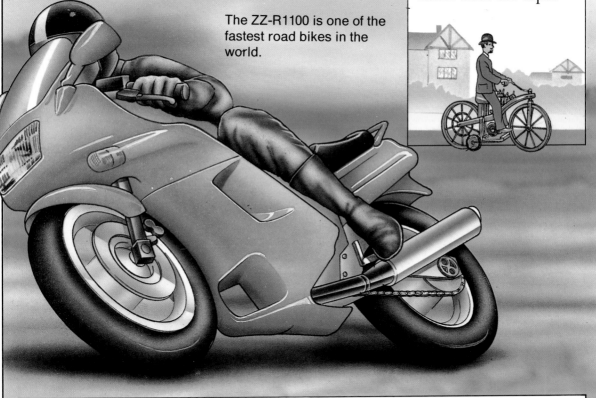

The ZZ-R1100 is one of the fastest road bikes in the world.

TEST-DRIVE BALL BEARINGS

Inside the wheels of bikes and cars are little metal balls called bearings, which help the wheels to spin around smoothly.

1 To see how bearings work, put some marbles in the rim of an empty can. Place a book on top and spin it gently.

2 Now try spinning the book without the marbles!

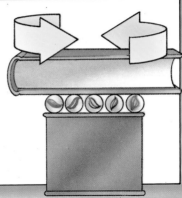

Who built the first locomotive?

The world's first working steam locomotive was built by Richard Trevithick of England. It made its first journey on February 13, 1804, along the rails of a Welsh mine track.

The first public railway, the Stockton and Darlington Railway in northeast England, opened in 1825. The steam locomotive below is the one that pulled the line's first train. It was called Locomotion and it was designed by George Stephenson.

STEAM FACTS

● Richard Trevithick's 1804 steam locomotive (above) covered nearly 10 miles on its first journey, at a speed of 5 mph.

● In 1829, Robert Stephenson's new locomotive Rocket achieved a top speed of 29 mph.

● The first French steam locomotive was built by Marc Séguin in 1829.

● The first US-built locomotive, Peter Cooper's Tom Thumb, had its first run on August 25, 1830.

On its first run in 1825, Stephenson's Locomotion hauled the owner's coach, 11 coal wagons, a wagon of flour, 20 wagons of guests and workmen, plus an extra 300 people who climbed on for the ride. It averaged 8 mph, but reached 15 mph downhill.

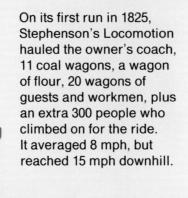

Which was the fastest steam train?

The fastest steam train was pulled by the British locomotive Mallard. In 1938 it reached nearly 130 mph, traveling slightly downhill. Mallard was pulling seven coaches weighing over 260 tons.

Which is the fastest electric train?

The fastest electric train is the French TGV, which set a record of 320 mph in 1990. West Germany's InterCity Express (ICE) can do 248 mph, while Britain's Intercity 225 can reach 140 mph.

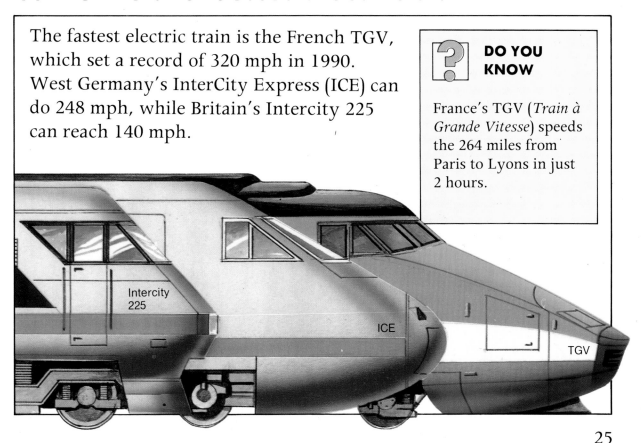

Intercity 225

ICE

TGV

Where is the world's longest railway?

The longest railway in the world runs across the USSR and is called the Trans-Siberian line. It is 5,864 miles long and was built in the 1890s across the frozen plains and thick forests of Siberia. The complete journey takes eight days, with 97 stops.

RAILWAY FACTS

● The longest straight line of track in the world runs for 297 miles across the Nullarbor Plain of western and southern Australia.

● Gauge is the distance between the rails of a railway track. Railways can be standard, narrow, or broad gauge. Standard gauge is 4 feet, $8\frac{1}{2}$ inches.

Where is the world's highest railway?

The world's highest standard-gauge railway is in South America, where the Central Railway of Peru climbs to 15,804 feet in the Andes Mountains. This is higher than the top of Mont Blanc, the highest peak in the European Alps.

DO YOU KNOW

The first railway to cross a continent was built across the USA between 1863 and 1869. It was 1,724 miles long.

What are monorails?

Mono means one, and monorails are trains that run on one rail, not two. The rail runs along a track that is usually well above the ground. Some monorail trains straddle the track and travel along the top of it. Others are suspended beneath the track. Monorails have been built in cities throughout the world, to carry people above streets busy with traffic. Others carry visitors through theme parks.

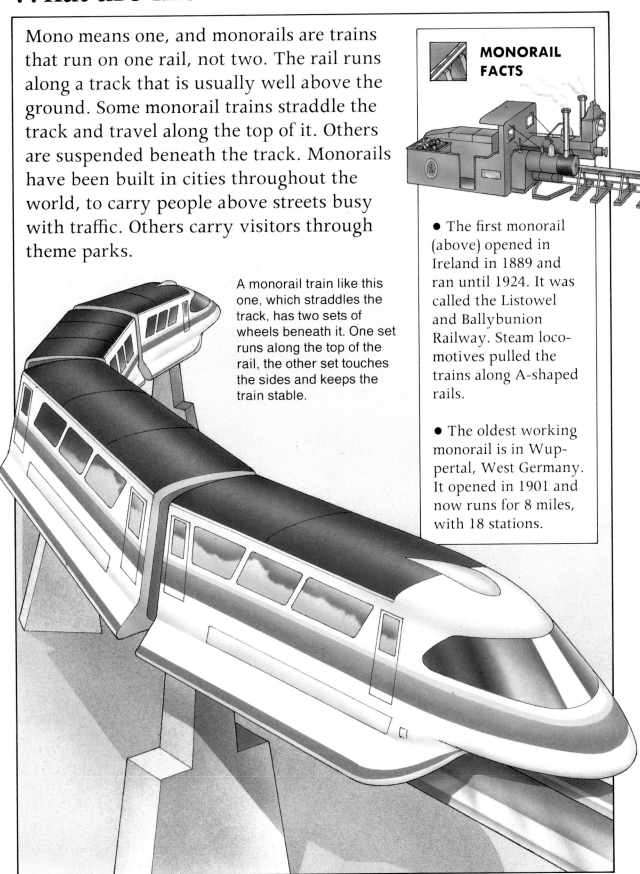

A monorail train like this one, which straddles the track, has two sets of wheels beneath it. One set runs along the top of the rail, the other set touches the sides and keeps the train stable.

MONORAIL FACTS

● The first monorail (above) opened in Ireland in 1889 and ran until 1924. It was called the Listowel and Ballybunion Railway. Steam loco-motives pulled the trains along A-shaped rails.

● The oldest working monorail is in Wuppertal, West Germany. It opened in 1901 and now runs for 8 miles, with 18 stations.

Which are the biggest ships?

The biggest ships in the world today are cargo vessels, such as oil tankers. These giant ships can be more than half a mile long and weigh around 440,000 tons.

The world's biggest passenger ship is a Norwegian cruise liner, *Sovereign of the Seas*, at 80,300 tons. The longest passenger ship in the world is the *Norway*, which is over 1,000 feet long.

DO YOU KNOW

Some tankers are so huge that the crew uses bicycles to get around the deck. A big tanker can take 20 minutes, and 5 miles, to stop!

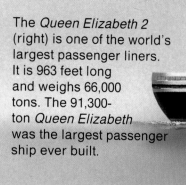

The *Queen Elizabeth 2* (right) is one of the world's largest passenger liners. It is 963 feet long and weighs 66,000 tons. The 91,300-ton *Queen Elizabeth* was the largest passenger ship ever built.

The world's longest aircraft carrier is the US Navy's *Enterprise* (below), at 1,112 feet. The US Navy's Nimitz class carriers are shorter, but heavier. Completed in 1960, *Enterprise* was the first nuclear-powered aircraft carrier.

WHY DO SHIPS FLOAT?

Ships only float if they weigh less than the amount of water they displace, or push aside.

1 You can see how this works by filling a bowl halfway with water.

Mark the water level on the bowl's sides. Use a metal or plastic food container as a ship, and put it into the water.

2 Now pour a little sand into your "ship" — it will sink farther into the water. As it does, it displaces some of the water — look at your original water level mark. If you overload your ship with sand it will sink.

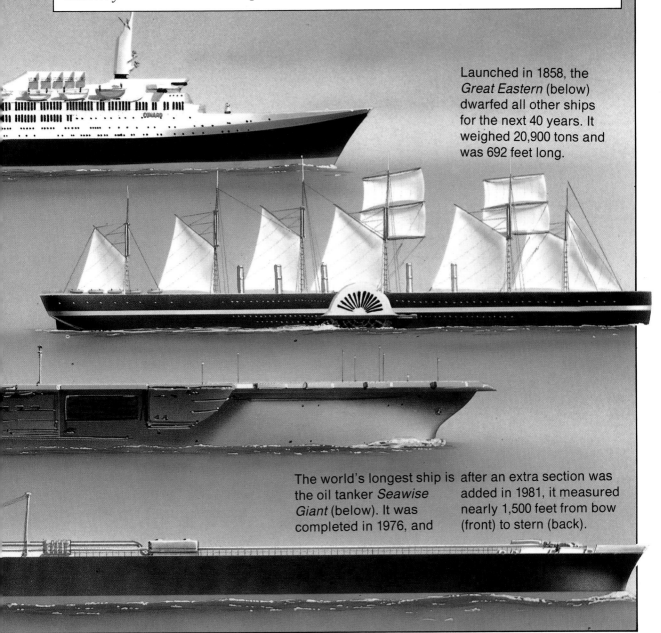

Launched in 1858, the *Great Eastern* (below) dwarfed all other ships for the next 40 years. It weighed 20,900 tons and was 692 feet long.

The world's longest ship is the oil tanker *Seawise Giant* (below). It was completed in 1976, and after an extra section was added in 1981, it measured nearly 1,500 feet from bow (front) to stern (back).

What were the first boats like?

People have been building and sailing boats for many thousands of years. The earliest and most simple type of boat was a flat raft made by lashing logs together. People also made canoes called dugouts, using fire and axes to hollow out tree trunks. Another early type of boat is the coracle. These small round boats were made by stretching animal skins over a lightweight wooden framework.

DO YOU KNOW

In 1970, a Norwegian named Thor Heyerdahl sailed a copy of an ancient Egyptian reed boat across the Atlantic Ocean in an attempt to prove that the Egyptians introduced reed boats to South America.

One of the earliest types of boat was a log raft (right). It was sturdy enough for crossing a river or a lake, but not for setting out to sea.

In the South Pacific, outrigger canoes similar to the one below have been used for ocean crossings for thousands of years.

Egyptian wall paintings made over 6,000 years ago show rafts like the one below. The ancient Egyptians built their rafts by lashing together bundles of a reed-like plant called papyrus.

Outrigger

Dugout canoe

How fast could sailing ships travel?

The fastest sailing ships were the clippers of the mid-1800s. These graceful cargo ships were designed for speed, with long, sleek bodies and many sails. In a strong wind, with all sails set, they could travel at over 20 mph. By the late 1800s, however, clippers had been overtaken by faster ships, which were powered by steam engines.

DO YOU KNOW

In 1866, the two clippers *Taeping* and *Ariel* raced from China to Britain in 99 days, and arrived only 20 minutes apart!

A typical clipper had three masts — the front one was called the foremast, the middle one was the mainmast, and the rear one was the mizzenmast. As many as 35 square sails could be set.

Mainmast

Mizzen-mast

Foremast

SAILING FACTS

● A clipper of the 1800s could cross the Atlantic in 12 days. The record crossing time for a modern passenger liner is just under $3\frac{1}{2}$ days.

● The biggest sailing ships of the 1800s were called windjammers. The largest, the *Preussen*, weighed 5,500 tons and had five masts.

● The longest distance covered under sail in one day was 532 miles by the clipper *Champion of the Seas* in 1854.

● The highest speed reached by any sailing craft is nearly 47 mph. This was set by a sail-board in 1988.

How do paddle-steamers work?

As their name suggests, these boats are powered by paddles and steam. The paddles are wide boards set into a large wheel, which is driven by a steam engine. As the wheel turns into the water, the paddles push against it. This makes the boat move. The earliest paddle-steamers had two wheels — one on either side of the center of the boat. Nowadays, most have a single large wheel at the back.

STEAMER FACTS

● The boat above was the first working paddle-steamer. It was built in the USA in 1787 by John Fitch.

● The world's largest inland boat is the paddle-steamer *Mississippi Queen*. This steamer is 380 feet long.

The first paddle-steamer trip down the Mississippi River took place in 1812. By 1846, nearly 1,200 steamers were working the river.

Paddle-steamers have large wheels driven by a steam engine. The paddles on the wheel move the boat, by pushing against the water.

Who sailed solo around the world first?

The first person to sail alone around the world was Joshua Slocum in 1895-1898. His yacht, *Spray*, was only 38 feet long.
The first nonstop, solo, around-the-world voyage was made by Robin Knox-Johnston in 1968–1969. He spent 312 days at sea in his boat *Suhaili*.

? DO YOU KNOW

The first around-the-world voyage, led by Spanish explorer Ferdinand Magellan, took place from 1519 to 1522.

Which is the fastest boat?

The world's fastest boat is Ken Warby's hydroplane *Spirit of Australia* (below). In 1977, this super-fast machine roared across a lake at 345 mph. The fastest speed reached by a powerboat is just over 228 mph.

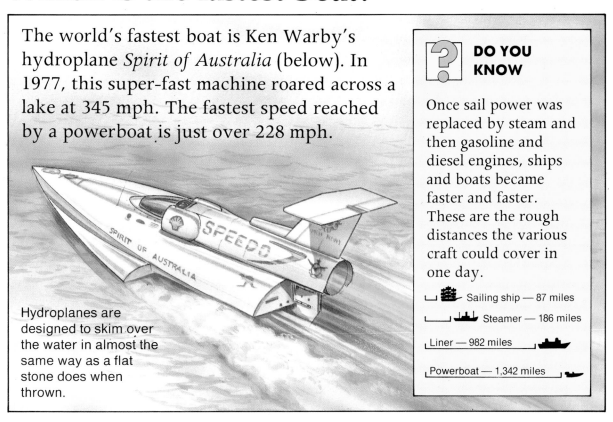

Hydroplanes are designed to skim over the water in almost the same way as a flat stone does when thrown.

? DO YOU KNOW

Once sail power was replaced by steam and then gasoline and diesel engines, ships and boats became faster and faster. These are the rough distances the various craft could cover in one day.

Sailing ship — 87 miles
Steamer — 186 miles
Liner — 982 miles
Powerboat — 1,342 miles

How do hovercraft hover?

Hovercraft skim across the surface of the water or the land on a cushion of air. Fans blow air downward, where it is trapped inside the flexible, or bendable, skirt that surrounds the hovercraft. Floating on this trapped cushion of air, the hovercraft is driven along by aircraft-type propellers.

DO YOU KNOW

The world hovercraft speed record is held by the US Navy's SES-100B. This test craft reached a speed of 106 mph in 1980.

Aircraft-style propellers provide thrust to drive the hovercraft along.

Hovercraft can carry passengers and cars inside them. They can travel faster than ordinary ships.

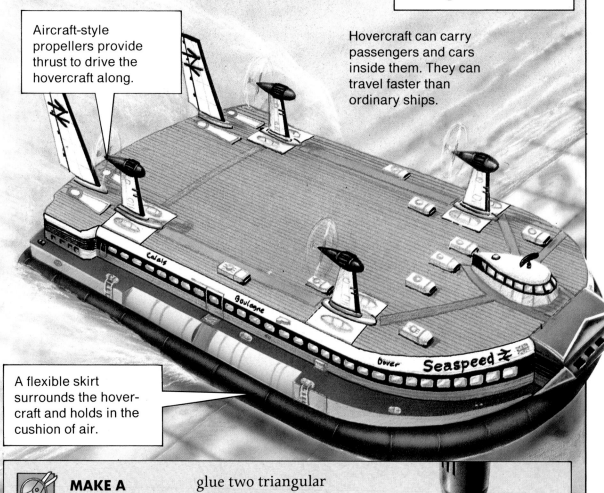

A flexible skirt surrounds the hovercraft and holds in the cushion of air.

 MAKE A HOVERCRAFT

1 Ask an adult to help you cut a hovercraft shape, with a hole about 2 inches across in the middle, out of a piece of polystyrene. Then glue two triangular pieces of thin wood on the back as rudders.

2 Put your hovercraft on a flat dry surface and use a hair dryer to blow air through the hole to make it float.

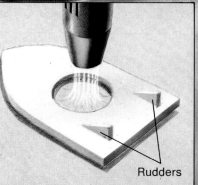

Rudders

What is a hydrofoil?

A hydrofoil is a boat whose hull, or body, can lift above the water when it is traveling at high speed. Most have two underwater wings called foils — one at the bow, or front, and one at the stern, or rear. As the hydrofoil builds up speed, it rises up on its foils and can skim over the water at speeds of 35 to 62 mph.

? DO YOU KNOW

The first successful hydrofoil was built by Enrico Forlanini of Italy in 1906. The hovercraft was invented in the 1950s by Christopher Cockerell of Britain.

1 When it isn't traveling at speed, a hydrofoil floats in the water just like any other boat (below).

2 As the hydrofoil gathers speed (right), it rises higher out of the water on its foils.

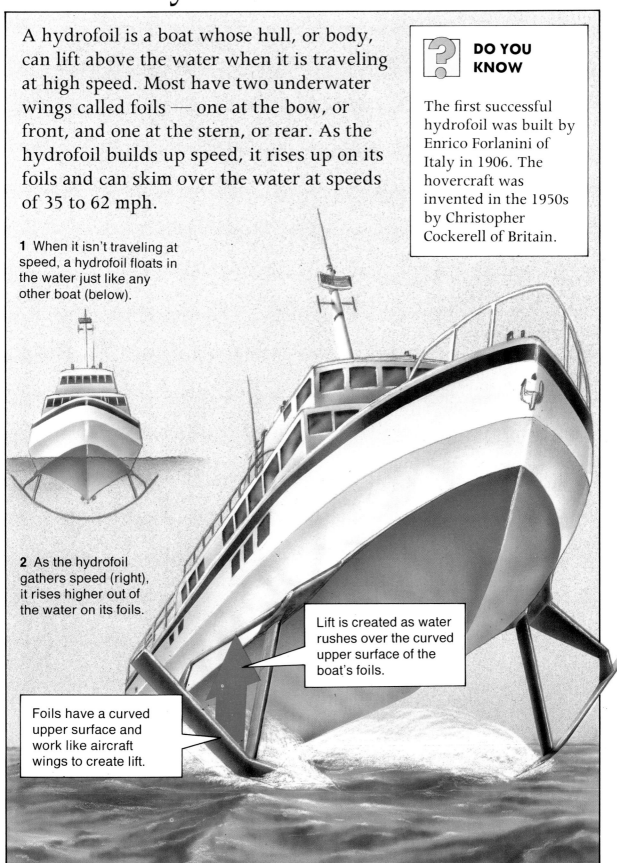

Lift is created as water rushes over the curved upper surface of the boat's foils.

Foils have a curved upper surface and work like aircraft wings to create lift.

How deep can submarines dive?

Most submarines cruise below the surface of the water at a depth of about 500 feet. Few can dive below 1,400 feet. This is because water has pressure, or push, which increases with depth. Deep below the surface of the ocean, the water pressure is enough to squash the steel hull of the average submarine as flat as a pancake!

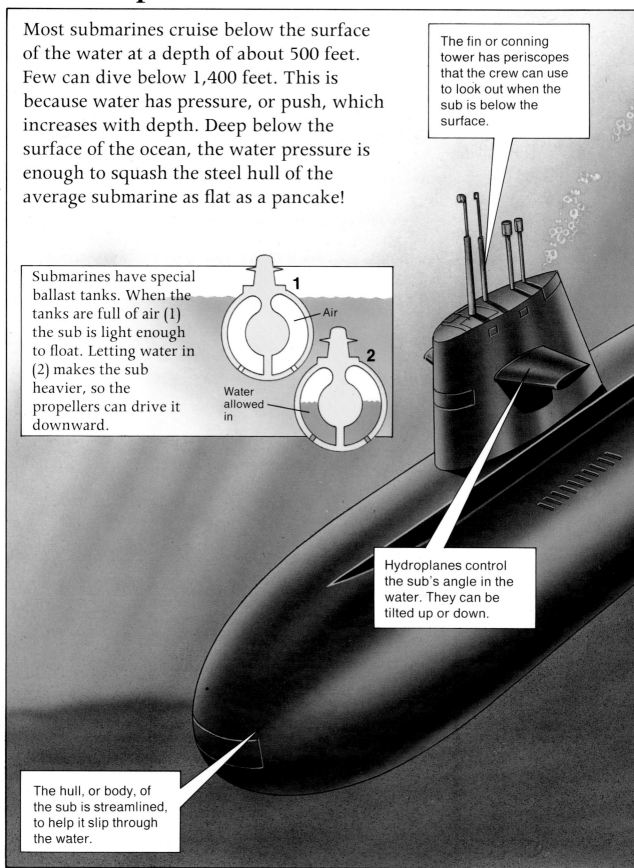

The fin or conning tower has periscopes that the crew can use to look out when the sub is below the surface.

Submarines have special ballast tanks. When the tanks are full of air (1) the sub is light enough to float. Letting water in (2) makes the sub heavier, so the propellers can drive it downward.

1

Air

2

Water allowed in

Hydroplanes control the sub's angle in the water. They can be tilted up or down.

The hull, or body, of the sub is streamlined, to help it slip through the water.

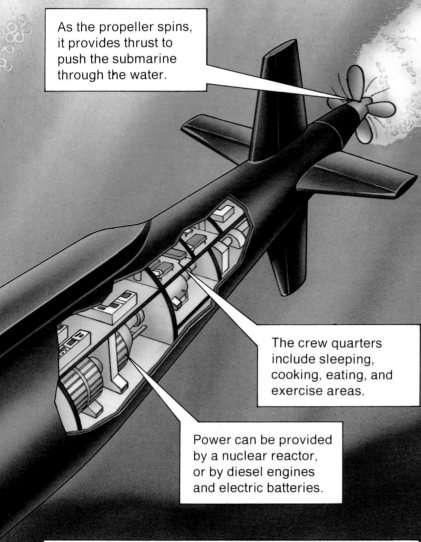

As the propeller spins, it provides thrust to push the submarine through the water.

The crew quarters include sleeping, cooking, eating, and exercise areas.

Power can be provided by a nuclear reactor, or by diesel engines and electric batteries.

 SUBMARINE FACTS

● The tiny *Turtle* (below) was the first submarine to be used in battle. In 1776, during the Revolutionary War, it was used to try to mine a British ship in New York harbor, but failed. One person sat inside and turned the propeller by hand to push it along.

Turtle

● The *Resurgam* (below) was built in 1879 and had a steam engine. Unfortunately, it sank with its crew on board.

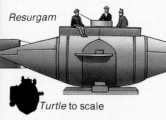

Resurgam

Turtle to scale

● The US inventor John P. Holland made the first successful submarine in 1897. Gasoline engines drove it on the surface. Underwater it ran on batteries.

 DO YOU KNOW

The *Trieste* (right) is a special kind of submarine called a bathyscaphe, which can cope with the enormous pressure of deep water. In 1960 it dived 36,000 feet into the deepest part of the Pacific Ocean. The cabin is in the ball underneath.

What will future travel be like?

One of the main changes in transportation will be in the fuel that's used. Nowadays, most vehicles get power from burning gasoline in an engine. But gasoline is made from oil, and the world's oil reserves are running out fast. Other, cleaner fuels must be found, since burning gasoline also produces gases that pollute, or dirty, the air.

Maglev trains are a new and very fast type of intercity transport. They float above the track on an invisible magnetic field.

New V/STOL designs include planes whose rotors tilt up for vertical take-off and landing, and forward for normal flight.

The sun's energy can be collected by special panels and used to make electricity to power small road vehicles and aircraft.

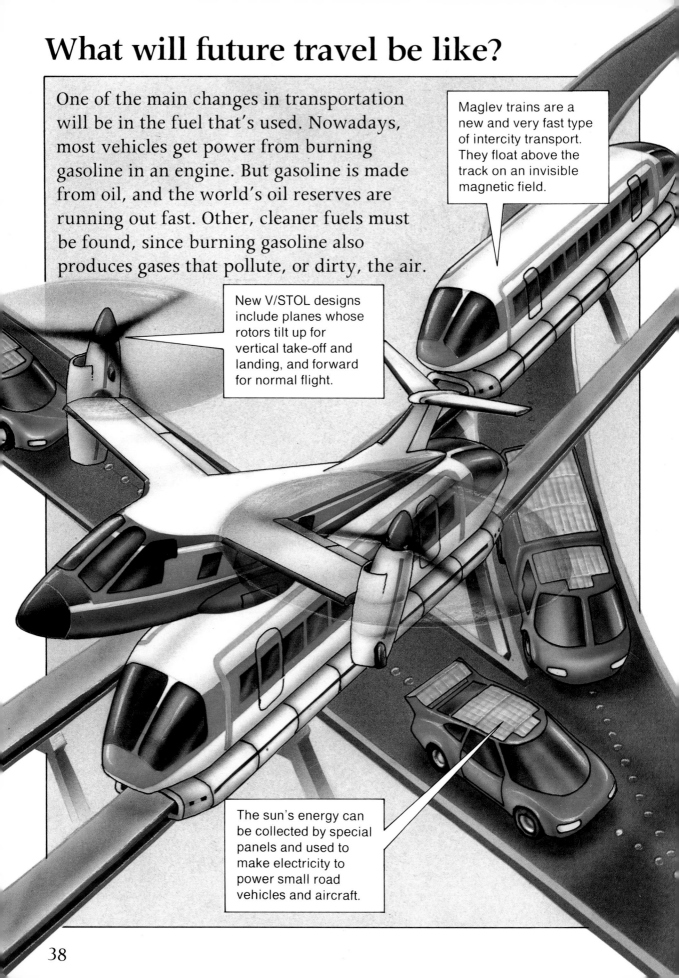

Useful words

Fuselage   The body of an airplane.

Gasoline engine   An engine in which gasoline and air are burned, producing hot gases. The gases force a piston up and down a cylinder inside the engine. A connecting rod and crankshaft then change this up-and-down movement to circular movement — the wheels go around and the car or other machine moves. Most car engines have four to six cylinders.

Jet engine   An engine in which fuel and oxygen (from air) are burned to make a jet of hot gases. The gases shoot backward out of the engine, producing thrust and propelling the machine forward.

Lift   The force that keeps an aircraft airborne. Air has pressure, or push, and lift is created by the difference in air pressure above and below the aircraft's wings. These must have a special shape called an airfoil, which is more curved above than below. The air flowing over an airfoil's curved upper surface moves faster and has less pressure than the air flowing beneath it. Water flowing over the curved foils of a hydrofoil also creates lift.

Locomotive   The part of a train that contains the engines and pulls the carriages.

Propel   Another word for push.

Rotor   The rotating, or spinning, part of a machine. The rotor of a helicopter consists of the spinning blades that give it lift.

Steam engine   An engine in which fuel such as coal or wood is burned to heat water in a boiler. When the water boils, it turns into steam, which is used to drive a piston backward and forward. Connecting rods and a crankshaft attached to the piston then change this back-and-forth movement into circular movement — the wheels go around and the locomotive or other machine moves.

Thrust   The force that pushes a machine forward. Modern aircraft are given thrust by their jet engines. The spinning propeller of a ship or submarine also creates thrust.

V/STOL   Short for "vertical/short take-off and landing."

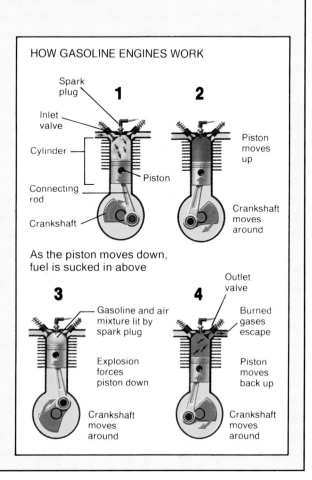

HOW GASOLINE ENGINES WORK

Spark plug · Inlet valve · Cylinder · Connecting rod · Piston · Crankshaft

1 · **2** Piston moves up · Crankshaft moves around

As the piston moves down, fuel is sucked in above

3 Gasoline and air mixture lit by spark plug · Explosion forces piston down · Crankshaft moves around

4 Outlet valve · Burned gases escape · Piston moves back up · Crankshaft moves around

Index